PRAISE FOR *DESIGNING THE BEST WORK-FROM-HOME YOU*

"Vennessa has taken one of the most challenging issues and delivered simple (yet elegant!) advice. Her pragmatic guidance on how to maximize your productivity while working from home is critical for many during the COVID-19 crisis. I've struggled immensely working from home with two kiddos and reading this book has been a LIFESAVER! Vennessa truly defines epic awesomeness!"

—*Dominic Vogel, founder and chief strategist, Cyber.SC*

"Working from home is quickly becoming a new normal for people. What isn't normal is knowing how to do it effectively and efficiently … until now. Thank you, Vennessa. This book is a game and life changer."

—*Anthony Trucks, former NFL player, American Ninja Warrior, international speaker, podcast host, and founder of Identity Shift Coaching*

"This book is a must read—a helpful guide for every leader and professional seeking work-life balance and productivity in the new normal where boundaries between home life and work life have been blurred."

—*Dr. Vivian O. Ikem, transformational coach, The Reset Squad & Podcast Host, NLP Certified Coach; John Maxwell Team Coach*

"Vennessa is one of those dynamic individuals that can do many things in an organized and structured way, whereas a lot of other people have trouble and difficulty focusing on just one. What I admire about her most is her willingness to want to see her clients and those that she inspires succeed with what they're looking to achieve in their businesses. When you have someone like Vennessa in your corner, who teaches you how to structure your day, stay organized, and create a work space at home that is conducive to success and prosperity, there is no wonder why this book is going to impact so many. Congratulations my friend. You truly inspire me and so many."

—*Scott Aaron, internationally acclaimed and award-winning network marketer, author, podcaster, and speaker*

DESIGNING
THE BEST WORK-FROM-HOME YOU

DESIGNING
THE BEST WORK-FROM-HOME YOU

HOW TO WORK REMOTELY (BUT NOT ALL THE TIME)

VENNESSA MCCONKEY

Advantage®

Published by Advantage, Charleston, South Carolina.
Member of Advantage Media Group.

ADVANTAGE is a registered trademark, and the Advantage colophon is a trademark of Advantage Media Group, Inc.

Printed in the United States of America.

10 9 8 7 6 5 4 3 2 1

ISBN: 978-1-64225-207-1
LCCN: 2020913159

Cover design by David Taylor.
Layout design by Carly Blake.

This publication is designed to provide accurate and authoritative information in regard to the subject matter covered. It is sold with the understanding that the publisher is not engaged in rendering legal, accounting, or other professional services. If legal advice or other expert assistance is required, the services of a competent professional person should be sought.

Advantage Media Group is proud to be a part of the Tree Neutral® program. Tree Neutral offsets the number of trees consumed in the production and printing of this book by taking proactive steps such as planting trees in direct proportion to the number of trees used to print books. To learn more about Tree Neutral, please visit **www.treeneutral.com**.

Advantage Media Group is a publisher of business, self-improvement, and professional development books and online learning. We help entrepreneurs, business leaders, and professionals share their Stories, Passion, and Knowledge to help others Learn & Grow. Do you have a manuscript or book idea that you would like us to consider for publishing? Please visit **advantagefamily.com** or call **1.866.775.1696**.

To my children, Ethan, Dominick, and Asher. You are my world. Even as difficult as it has been some days working from home with you all around and being the crazy kids you are, I wouldn't trade these days for any corporate office gig. You all brighten up my day, and I'm so blessed that God gave me all three of you! I love you all.

To my husband, Matt. Thank you for supporting me on this intense yet fulfilling journey, the long days and nights and the sacrifices you have made to help me fulfill God's will. Love you.

CONTENTS

INTRODUCTION

FINDING CLARITY AND CONFIDENCE WHEN WORKING AND LEADING FROM HOME

There was a time before COVID-19 when I'd take the kids to the YMCA, where they had two hours of childcare—provided that a parent was in the building. So not only could I work out if I needed to, but I could also work and take uninterrupted client calls. I was able to get some writing done, and the kids were able to be interactive and social. Afterward, my oldest would go to school, leaving me with two rather than three kids the rest of my workday, and the three of us had our own schedules, which involved their naps.

Fast-forward to the great work-from-home push

powered by the coronavirus. Not only is there no school, but there's also no open YMCA. There's no coffee shop escape. There's a sudden lack of routine, and gone are those breaks that allow me time to think and properly work. All of a sudden, the kids are bombing Zoom calls, making funny faces behind my back. Oh, and did I mention that now my husband is also using our home as an office space?

A work-from-home veteran, I quickly discovered all-new challenges to having a remote work space: the lack of boundaries, space, and breaks, to name a few. It's dizzying just thinking about it.

A NEW NORMAL

We are frazzled when we are exhausted (we can't even catch up on rest or get breaks like we used to), and it's hard to be empathetic (we can't "fake" it when we're surrounded by the ones we love the most and drive us crazy nonstop). And it's even more difficult to make the space and time for creative thought without interruptions—especially if you have children. All of these stressors have implications for business and worker productivity during this new #WFH normal.

Even as a parent who worked at home for five years, I used to have time where I could take the kids to the gym, drop them off at school, or utilize a babysitter. The coronavirus shift, however, has presented a learning curve. Schedules and routines and planned-out quiet times have become imperative for all of us to stay sane. Business meetings with teams and clients now include at least two interruptions per thirty-minute meeting, along with some random child comment or toy thrown. And let's be real here: the mute button has allowed us to yell some statements back at our children, like "Be quiet! Mommy only has a few more minutes!" or "Mommy is on an important call—go play with your toys," or "Yes, go ahead and have the one hundredth snack for the day." And that's just before 10:00 a.m.

The business world has completely shifted, with a new mindset taking hold. But this isn't the first time we've had to adjust. Before the last several decades of telecommuting appeared, even going back hundreds of years, working from home was the only way. Combining work space and living space was a natural way for families and communities to efficiently pool resources, make the most of the space at hand, and work cooperatively together for the good of all. Are we actually thinking of working from home in these terms? Or are we bothered by our children and spouses?

In medieval times, the working classes set up craft- and trade-focused shops in their homes, offering goods and services to support their families in living spaces that were architecturally designed to accommodate working from home. For example, their single-story, one-roomed homes were a combination of kitchen and spinning/weaving/dressmaking workshops, plus bedroom, dining room, butchery, and so forth. And what did that mean for those at home? Multitasking. Managing resources and finances. The division of labor. Teaching and managing the children. Boundaries between home and work life, if they existed at all, were blurred at best.

It wasn't until the twentieth century that the "office" became the norm, ultimately separating work and family. Right or wrong, this is how most business began to be conducted. Now, it seems like we are back in time, and it's probably for the best too.

I think too many of us believed that teachers, childcare workers, and educators were supposed to be dealing with our kids during the day and teaching them most of what they should know, with us as parents reinforcing it during the three to five hours we may have with them each day. Now, the extra time at home with the family has reintroduced many of us to what it's like to simply be with the ones we love rather than rush through the evenings in a flurry of homework, dinners, baths, and bedtimes. Working from home, it turns out, really does have its unexpected benefits.

WFH, A GIFT?

Yes, a gift—in more ways than one. From an employee's perspective, for example, being at home enables us to connect more with our families and even our communities as we reach out to help neighbors who may be elderly or have health issues.

Even after COVID-19 is long gone, companies will remember the benefits they experienced, which is why many believe that this really is the new normal: that working from home is, in many cases, an improvement and the way forward.

> **Working from home is, in many cases, an improvement and the way forward.**

Businesses now realize they can reduce overhead with a smart work-from-home structure. And companies are learning that in order to stand out more, they must be flexible and empathetic with employees, driving productivity while not increasing hours of work. What we are all realizing is that the workday can be a different and much better experience. Working from home may seem strange or difficult to adjust to, but once it's mastered, you'll see why it really is a game changer.

That's what I hope to do in this book. I want to show you all the ways that the new work-from-home normal is a fresh mindset and a unique opportunity. This is coming from someone who, again, has done the whole work-from-home life long before the #WFH hashtag existed.

WHERE I'M COMING FROM

My parents and both sets of grandparents were business owners who worked from home. My dad's dad was a surgical eye instrument maker, and my grandma (his wife) was his secretary. They had very clear start and stop times and defined breaks for naps, snacks, lunch, and *Wheel of Fortune*! My mom's parents? Same thing, except my grandpa worked as much as he could in his shop on cars to avoid the arguments with Grandma.

On the other side of the coin, my dad had a carpet cleaning business out of our home and worked like a dog with no clearly defined start and stop times. We never knew when Dad would be home for any meal, which meant him showing up at 7:00 p.m. or much later as we were washing dishes. Once we girls were out of the house, Mom started her naturopathic practice, and we rarely saw either parent. We would go to their house during the day, and no one would show up for hours. We would say we were coming over for dinner, only to be told that they would have to take a rain check even though we had already cleared our evenings. Even on the days they were doing office admin work from home, they always seemed too busy to really be present.

What I learned from all of these experiences growing up is that each set of family members was absolutely working their hardest to provide for their families, using their gifts and talents God gave them. But the biggest takeaway I saw was that the ones who had defined routines and respected themselves, their work, and their families enough ended up having healthier mental and physical lives—and actually made more money and remained without debt. So I have been extremely blessed to, first, have noticed all of this, and second, have a crazy type-A, very disciplined personality that keeps me and my family on track, as well as now many others, in both my personal and professional life.

That's why I'm a career coach. It made sense to utilize those strengths and skills I've picked up from both my family as well as my years in corporate settings and follow my calling to become an entrepreneur. With a background in operations management, engineering, and marketing, I've helped hundreds of people gain new employment and confidence in who they are. You can trust me because I've been there, in search of clarity, focus, and confidence in my career and life. On top of being a mother to three boys, I also battle depression and major health issues, so I understand that *life* can alter your path. I'm here to help you navigate that and, ultimately, design the best you.

LET'S DESIGN THE BEST YOU

Whether you are working from home temporarily during a particularly stressful time or you're in it for the long haul, this book will show you that working from home can be a blessing—but only if you use the gift appropriately. You'll learn everything from time-management tips that will make you more productive and give you more personal time to advice on how to respect your family enough to look up from your computer when a child or spouse walks into your office space. I'll show you the importance of taking care of your mental and physical health during any point in the day by eating healthier, moving your body, writing out thoughts that are troublesome, and more. You'll have the clarity and confidence to work and lead effectively from afar and transform your quality of life so that you can be your very best you—your extraordinary you—both in and out of the home office.

Are you ready? Let's go!

CHAPTER I

THE WFH ENVIRONMENT: ARE YOU SET UP FOR SUCCESS?

Have you ever scavenged something useful from the side of the road? Regardless of how you feel about picking, you may appreciate that my husband once happened upon a really cool, old, massive wooden spool. When I looked at it, I saw so much more than a secondhand spool—I could see the possibilities beyond its state of disrepair. Knowing that the top circular part would make a great desktop, I sawed part of that flat so it could stand up flush against my bedroom wall. I took the whole thing apart, sanded it down, and painted it.

Now it has legs and a comfortable chair to go with it. Atop the upcycled spool sits pictures my kids have drawn me, a salt lamp, and a diffuser that emanates uplifting citrus scents in the morning and calming lavender essential oil as the day winds down. There's also room for a laptop, my morning coffee, and my podcast mic. I have a spot for my phone and plenty of room to move. A nearby box on the floor contains additional needs: notebooks, extra technology, cords, plugins, pens (yes, those have to stay hidden from my adorable but thieving children!). My corner office is full of weird little things that make me smile; it's my very own environment.

That's what this chapter is all about, helping you to set up your physical home office space, your own environment that is uniquely designed for and by you and your specific needs. One thing that is important to keep in mind as you go about creating this space is that, like all environments, it's subject to change. What works at first will inevitably shift as our lives and surroundings evolve.

As I write to you, it is early morning, and I'm situated in that special corner of my bedroom where I set up my uniquely me work-from-home space years ago when I made the move from the corporate life to an entrepreneurial one. Even though I'm what I would consider a WFH veteran, I, too, was thrown a curveball with COVID-19 and had to make some minor adjustments to how I approached my personal office space. From the early days of freelance to recently, I didn't just work at my house. If I wasn't set up at the YMCA, it was Panera Bread or a coffee shop. My office was, really, my briefcase. Laptop, notebooks, planner, highlighters, snacks—everything an on-the-go pro could need for a mobile office. But at home, I could work in my bedroom corner office. I could also pop up at a different desk in our home that is now not only the baby's room but also my husband's new post-COVID work-from-home space. Some couples can work in the same room and feed off one another, but that's not how we work—one of the many recent discoveries in this new normal of working from home.

There's a lot to learn about working from home, but first things first. Let's set you up for success by setting up that physical WFH space, beginning with finding a dedicated space in your home where all the magic is going to happen!

FIND A DEDICATED SPACE

No one expects you to suddenly have a room all to yourself that solely serves as an office. We have to work with what we have, right? When determining which nook of your house your "office" will occupy, ensure that the space is quiet and has good lighting. Avoid the centerpieces of the household, rooms where things tend to get loud (like the kitchen, dining room, or living room). A nice light will energize you, so if you can't find good lighting, consider something like a ring light.

Quiet space and light are two things that will serve you well when it comes to concentration and good energy, but they're also going to go a long way on video calls. If possible, your space should also have a good background for those Zoom calls, but if that isn't possible, remember you can always hang a white sheet behind you and use a special Zoom background.

THE DESK SETUP: EVERYTHING HAS ITS PLACE

Your actual desk, if at all possible, should not be the kitchen or coffee table. A more permanent space is crucial for your mindset, so use what you have (or can scavenge!) for a desk. You don't need something massive, but ideally you should have ample space for a laptop, notebook, and drink. One thing I'm big on (my engineering and manufacturing background is showing!) is *everything has its place*. Set yourself up for success by making sure your essential tools—pens, headphones, whatever—live somewhere, that they're accessible and easy to find when you need them. When you have a consistent system in place, you'll have less chaos, less stress.

Make sure your desk allows you room to move.

> **When you have a consistent system in place, you'll have less chaos, less stress.**

Being Italian and German, I need room to move. I get up, I talk with my hands. Sometimes I'm hitting the table, and it's moving. So I have to have space to be able to get up and move around too.

CARE ABOUT YOUR CHAIR

Getting a comfortable chair with a supportive back is really important. Make sure you're always sitting up. So many times, especially when we're at home, we lounge. We cross our legs or we sit on our legs, putting our bodies in a posture. I learned from my chiropractor that it's unhealthy to sit and stay in a posture our bodies aren't designed for—it's how we get misaligned and sore and lose sleep. Try to sit up straight without your back resting on anything, shoulders down and relaxed. And don't just sit there for hours on end, either! You need to stand up, stretch, and move around occasionally no matter how good your chair is.

CHECK YOUR TECH

Double-check your internet connectivity, particularly for crucial video calls. Download essential apps like Zoom onto both your laptop and phone—make sure you can switch to your phone if something goes wrong, for example, on your laptop. Your screen is going to freeze; it's inevitable. Be able to have grace and laugh when it does, for yourself and for your employees.

SET UP YOUR "HYDRATION STATION"

Hydrate! No, you don't need that water refilling station like you had at the office, but a good refillable water bottle will serve you just as well. Get a water bottle that you love, something that you'll like looking at on your desk, and make it a part of your work station. It's so easy to get caught up and forget to fuel up, but a little bit of water will go a long way in making sure your brain is good to go. Water delivers nutrients to the brain and removes toxins, meaning you'll be much more mentally alert and effective when hydrated.

GET EQUIPPED

What do you need to feel totally confident in your home office space? I recommend noise-canceling headphones as well as quality speakers on your computer. Some people work better with a second screen, which you can easily order online and hook up to your laptop. Even just having a much bigger screen than the laptop screen can be a total game changer and help you feel more confident in your WFH space.

PERSONALIZE YOUR SPACE

Make your space all yours. Whether it's framed photos, pictures your kids have drawn, or plants, add things to your desk, without cluttering it, that make you smile. Plants or flowers are great because they add oxygen to your space, boosting your mood and improving cognitive function. On my desk, I have a salt lamp that I believe has similar benefits. It's nice to look at and relaxes me. It makes me smile.

CREATE A PHYSICAL SEPARATION BETWEEN WORK AND HOME

Separate home and work life with a dedicated start and stop time. You can create that much-needed mental and physical shutdown with your work space by simply having strict office hours. Signal the start of your day with the ceremonial opening of your laptop. Miss the rush of walking out of your office door at 5:00 p.m.? You can get that same euphoric high from closing your laptop! Even better, shut off that screen, put your phone down for a moment, and immediately go for a tech-free walk to add physical distance from work. If you have kids, they'll be chomping at the bit to go play, forcibly reminding us adults that it's time to stop and "smell the roses."

Whatever you do, don't let your days bleed into nights. Be disciplined with what time you arrive and depart your dear, dedicated WFH space.

Now that you're set up for WFH success, let's talk about what leadership looks like when you're doing it from a distance. Hint: You'll want to find the perfect Zoom background!

ACTION STEPS

- Start thinking about the best possible nook in your home that ticks all the boxes for getting set up for success.

- Already have a good WFH spot? What can you do to make it a place that gives you more confidence? A better chair? A new plant? Sometimes a good decluttering is the best place to start!

- Delve in a little more. I have plenty more WFH advice on my blog at **vennessamcconkey.com**!

CHAPTER 2

LEADING REMOTELY: TIPS ON MANAGING A TEAM FROM A DISTANCE

One of my clients (we'll call him Thomas) has been having trouble in his new management role. It's not easy to get comfortable with a new team and role, much less when it's from afar. He'd already enlisted my career coaching services before COVID-19 happened in hopes of upleveling his career. His company was already working in silos, and he was trying to break those silos down but didn't know how. When everyone got moved to work from home, I could hear the panic in his voice: How was he supposed to manage people who already didn't quite respect him? His employees didn't want to show their faces on Zoom calls and didn't want to help each other out. In addition, he was dealing with assisting in the daily lives of his two little girls and feeling the stress of having to relieve his wife and do some needed home projects.

These days, working from home requires a more nuanced and flexible type of leadership. There are fresh but not-so-unusual ways to make sure you're leading your team from a place of clarity and confidence while leaving room for a life outside of work. Even before us all having to work from home, people were feeling undervalued in their jobs, like they were just a number. Now they have added stressors (that they may or may not disclose to their managers/ leaders), and it's your job to make sure their jobs won't break them.

Working and leading from home is a new normal, and everyone is on the same learning curve. That's what Thomas soon found out, and that's what this chapter is all about: learning how to navigate this new future of business that's conducted from afar.

REALIZE THAT THE EIGHT-HOUR WORKDAY IS A MYTH

Most people still feel they have to work a full eight hours or they'll get in trouble. They then take on projects and tasks to feel important and not lose their jobs. How can you ease that stress?

Realize that the eight-hour workday is a myth. No one really works that way—office days are full of little breaks, including an hour of lunch. Don't forget to take those at home and to encourage your staff to as well.

Don't believe that you need to be *on* all the time, or *busy*. We wear ourselves out! And when we're depleted, our creativity and our ability to innovate in moments of crisis go away. Communicate to your staff about what chunks of the day would be your best, as well as their best, available hours. Some work better in the early morning hours, while some work better later at night. If they communicate those things, then everyone knows what is going on, and it allows each person to be themselves and tend to their personal lives as well.

Encourage your employees to pretend like they are going to the office each day. Get up early. Work out. Shower. Eat. Get dressed in something other than comfy clothes. We're happier and more productive when we feel good about ourselves and our appearance.

ADJUST YOUR EXPECTATIONS

This new normal is also about respecting the fact that employees are in their home. You can call them, but don't get mad if they don't answer right away because they may be dealing with a situation at home. Or someone's kid may interrupt your Zoom call—that's OK! Things come up, so we have to give grace and we have to communicate. It's simple.

For example, if employees have young kids at home, suggest virtual playdates while their parents are on a Zoom meeting. Include the kids in on a meeting, and let them know it's OK if they interrupt. Provide them with fun activities during the workday, like a team workout, and create a minichallenge around those activities.

I always have a box of "quiet time" toys and activities. My boys know these are for special times and look forward to when they can play with these items. It also reduces the opportunity for me to just put them in front of the TV during important calls.

DISTINGUISH TEAM PERSONALITIES

Honing in on employees' differing personalities is key to managing them from a distance. For example, if you have a team member who loves to talk and needs to talk (those high extroverts), how will you engage them without stressing them out because they don't have people physically near them to talk to? How will you get the introverts to talk so they get the connection the human brain needs on top of ensuring they don't get overworked and stressed from not being able to recover properly from all the back-to-back Zoom meetings?

> **Honing in on employees' differing personalities is key to managing them from a distance.**

If you are a leader, knowing the personality type and work ethic of each of your team members is imperative whether you are in an office or working remotely. Keeping an extrovert in a closed-office setting with no one to talk to is going to stress them out. As a leader, it's not your job to do a specific job. It's your job to ensure your team members are doing their jobs in the best way they can. Tip: I delve further into the importance of knowing each of your team members' personality types on both my blog and podcast!

CLEARLY COMMUNICATE PRIORITIES AND TASKS

We are all in nonverbal mode. We have to make sure we're aligned and on the same page because we all interpret things differently. Emails, phone calls, and even video calls remove much of the nuance from how we communicate. As leaders, we need to over-communicate to our teams together and individually. Video meetings at least once a week are important. Use collaboration tools like Slack, Asana, and Google Calendar. Using whatever tools you choose, clearly outline tasks according to priority.

Remember, everything may appear urgent, but not everything has the same urgency. Prioritize between what is truly important for the business, for your employees, and what appears incredibly urgent.

ASSIGN INDIVIDUAL KPIS

Managers and workers alike need to get crystal clear on precisely what constitutes success for every single team member. Regardless of their position, every employee should have at least one key performance indicator (KPI) that reflects how well they're doing their job.

For customer service reps, for example, these KPIs would include customer feedback ratings to indicate the quality of their service and the total number of customers served to indicate the quantity. Without clear expectations and KPIs, neither you nor your employer can know how you perform. And without that knowledge, your job security becomes flimsy since you can't point to hard evidence of your performance.

PRIORITIZE AND STICK TO IT

Make a list of the daily activities you have to do, the ones that are routine and if they don't get done, someone will be after you. Then you have your top three priorities that will advance your role. Break those down into smaller tasks and work on those until those priorities are done (more tips on my favorite process in staying motivated and efficiently productive in the next chapter!).

TRUST YOUR TEAM, AND ALLOW THEM TO DISCONNECT

Trust your team but adjust expectations. This is an opportunity to work on micromanagement tendencies. If you've clearly outlined priorities, tasks, and deadlines, trust the team to succeed.

> **If you've clearly outlined priorities, tasks, and deadlines, trust the team to succeed.**

And allow them to disconnect—force them to! Our best ideas tend to come to us when we aren't working, like during a shower, meditation, or bike ride. We need to be disconnected. One of the fundamental delusions that has been driving us all is that in order to be successful, we basically need to be *on* all the time. Our employees need to be given permission to speak up and tell us what they need. And that means if a child suddenly needs their mom or dad (your staff member), then that employee needs to feel that they have the permission to reach out to their manager and say that they will be offline for whatever reason.

SET AN AGENDA FOR VIDEO MEETINGS

There should be a clear start and stop time and an agenda you stick to during Zoom calls. Make sure that any concerns that aren't discussed in the call are addressed in an email directly after the call. If further actions are required, make sure there's a follow-up email. When in doubt, overcommunicate! And make sure you've all agreed to the same time zone. Oh, and speaking of Zoom, don't forget to arrange an appropriate background for your calls—lead by example and steer clear of clutter, choosing a blank wall, bookshelf, or an appropriate digital background.

COMMUNICATE ANY ISSUES

You have to communicate performance, good and bad. That's a hard one. I don't know about you, but it's already awkward enough being on a video call and you're talking to a screen, and you have to sit there and tell them, "Hey, you're doing a terrible job," and you can't quite read all of the nonverbal communication that they have. You can't see that they're crossing their legs and twitching—that's all gone when you just have a face or an upper body on a screen. The solution?

Ask questions and really dig in as leaders. Take extra time to investigate what's going on there and have a one-on-one video call to address any issues.

CHECK IN ON EMPLOYEES

Check in and do something nice for your employees. Even just sending little notes can be encouragement enough, but you could also send a gift card for coffee or a little something from Etsy. How many of us, now working at home, get excited to go get the mail? It's an event! Sometimes even a kind, short email or text shows you care outside of the work environment and can be *just* what a person needs to get through the rest of the day.

We need community more than ever now. If you see employees struggling, reach out, arrange a video call, and show some support. That's what Thomas did. One-on-one video calls helped establish a better rapport with those he hadn't gotten to know well in person yet, and it ensured everyone had clarity and was on the same page.

Need advice on how to stay motivated at home? Keep going—that's what the next chapter is all about!

ACTION STEPS

- If you haven't already, schedule the most important Zoom conference you'll have: the one where you let everyone know that you realize that these times call for flexibility. Reassure them that no one works for eight hours, and that the team can stay on task and build even more efficiently now.

- Send an encouraging card or email to a team member you're pretty proud of.

- Schedule a one-on-one with a member who you're concerned about.

CHAPTER 3

FINDING YOUR FOCUS: HOW TO STAY MOTIVATED AT HOME

Most of my clients struggle at first when it comes to motivation when working at home. One client, Linda, thought she had a great routine down but was never able to wind down at night. She found it hard to differentiate her work life from her home life, with the days bleeding into the night in what turned out to be an aimless "routine." At night, her brain wouldn't turn off, and she was losing sleep. Something had to give. That's when she came to me and we got her more organized. We created boundaries and talked through ways to stay motivated and focused during her work hours so that when 5:00 p.m. came, she could confidently shut down her computer, as well as her brain, giving her a great work-life balance. She knew her focus had properly shifted to the right priorities. She was abundantly productive with her day—she could rest easy.

That's what we'll do here, too: teach you how to focus, stay motivated, and accomplish the day's tasks amid the distractions at home. Don't be too hard on yourself if this is a big struggle for you—you are most certainly not alone!

RISE EARLY (OR AT LEAST EARLIER)

Wake up earlier than normal and start doing what needs to be done without any further procrastination. It's that simple. We all get down from time to time—I get that. But we need to level up and stop waiting to *feel* motivated or inspired to get started! Having that time to yourself before the rest of the world starts moving can be such a productive time. You can hear yourself think without an

> Start taking a more mature approach to your overall performance by making it a way of life.

onslaught of emails to interrupt you. It's a great time to get a few things out of the way—like your workout, a meditation, or journaling—so you can focus on work priorities.

Start taking a more mature approach to your overall performance by making it a way of life, the way you carry yourself and the way in which you operate—then you won't need to get hyped up and motivated every three minutes just to do the things you should already be doing! You'll be more in control and calmly going about your business and getting big things done without the noise.

GET DRESSED

Of course it sounds fun, in theory, to work in your pj's just because you *can,* but dressing for the day in something other than a baseball hat or yoga pants is going to make you feel more motivated. When you feel good, you simply perform better. Dressing the part is a person's opportunity to set the tone for the day—will you be French toast (sweet and nicely put together) or burnt toast (crumbly and scattered all over the place)?

TRY THE POMODORO TECHNIQUE

The Pomodoro Technique is a game changer. Coined in the 1980s by Francisco Cirillo, the Pomodoro

Technique is an interval-focused method and can be the key to staying motivated. Here's how it works: make a list of tasks that need to be accomplished (more on making lists in a minute), and set a timer for every twenty-five minutes to complete a task. Once the timer goes off, take a small five-minute break and then set the timer and move on to the next task. After four of those tasks, take a longer fifteen to thirty-minute break.

I'm big on productivity and focused time. What I love about this technique is that the timer instills a sense of urgency. Rather than feeling like you have endless time in the workday to get things done and then ultimately squandering those precious work hours, you know you only have twenty-five minutes to make as much progress on a task as possible.

This method is a great start to those of us who think that sitting in front of a computer for three to four hours at a time without a break actually works. Our bodies need breaks! This technique forces you to be insanely focused and then get up and stretch your body, eyes, and mind, which is necessary. You can use those five-minute Pomodoro breaks to throw a load of laundry in, refill your coffee or water, do a quick meditation, play with your animals or kids, or simply stretch your muscles a little.

At the end of the day, you actually feel better, like you actually put in an honest day's work, and you tend to feel less stressed, blurry-eyed, and cramped up. Go figure—actually standing up a couple of times throughout the day really helps.[1]

MAKE LISTS

Back to making lists. To really stay on top of your week, try making lists on Sunday—that way you're ready to hit the ground running on Monday. I suggest making three different types of lists: one for long-term projects, one for short-term projects, and one for daily things needing to get done.

First, separate them into home things and work things. Then look at both lists and pull three items in total onto your top priority list for the day. This can be highly motivating, as you get to cross things off a list! You can even set a reward system for yourself and not have to depend on a team or department to pat you on the back at work.

---

1   You can learn more about the Pomodoro Technique in my blog post at https://blog.vennessamcconkey.com/blogs/news/big-key-to-help-you-focus.

FIND OUT WHAT WORK TRULY ENERGIZES YOU

We each have things that drain us and energize us. Take the ones that energize you and make sure at least one of them is on your list for the day. This gives you something to look forward to and, again, gives that sense of accomplishment. Communicate to keep your boss in the loop on things that energize and drain you too. Then they will know that if they give you a bunch of things that drain you, you won't be super motivated that day. This gives your boss the opportunity to mix things up too!

BUILD IN REWARDS

After you identify the work that energizes you, you'll still need to find ways to power through the ones you enjoy less but are still expected of you. Make these tasks feel like less of a chore by building in rewards of what you'll get to do once you check them off.

For example, when you feel unmotivated to complete a daunting task on your plate, tell yourself that you can enjoy a walk with your dog as soon as you get it done. That could also mean rewarding yourself with time to sit outside, work out, listen to a podcast, or play with your kids. Those Pomodoro breaks are great opportunities to build rewards into your day.

SET YOURSELF UP PHYSICALLY

Remote work can affect your mood and motivation to do anything productive. Again, as much as possible, try to maintain a separate work space so you can physically and mentally disconnect outside of work hours. Try to change up your posture every hour to reduce back, neck and shoulder pain. For example, you might start your day at your work desk, then transition to a standing position. Take breaks to stretch, rest your eyes away from the screen, and mentally recharge throughout the day. You can even put sticky note reminders on your desk or laptop to tell you to get up. I even like putting reminders on my phone.

> **As much as possible, try to maintain a separate work space so you can physically and mentally disconnect outside of work hours.**

PRACTICE SELF-COMPASSION

We all have off-days and things we are dealing with—that's OK! We all have things we are dealing with. Give yourself grace. For example, I have a couple of rare autoimmune diseases that literally knock me off my feet multiple days a month. It took me a few years to realize that it's OK and that's a sign that my body needs a break. When we go hard for so long, we lose focus, attention, etc., and our productivity declines; we aren't as happy. Do what your body and mind need to rejuvenate so you can be your best for others, even if that means a 1:00 p.m. catnap!

My biggest piece of advice here is to rejuvenate in a healthy way. Don't always veg in front of the TV and eat junk food. Be kind to your body.

LIMIT YOUR NEWS CONSUMPTION

For people like my husband, who has a journalism background, this is a hard one. It's OK to check the news from whatever outlet you follow, but set a time limit for that. The same rule applies to social media, TV, or any kind of media in general—set a timer if you have to and refocus on what's important to you when the timer goes off. If you need more social media discipline, try an app that blocks your biggest distractors for you.

Remember, you are not alone. Working from home is an all-new frontier for so many, a large chunk of whom are struggling along with you. Getting a new routine down and learning to stay focused in a new work environment is going to take practice, so don't give up. And don't miss the next chapter, which highlights mistakes to avoid when working from home. I hope you find further motivation there too.

ACTION STEPS

- Try rising early tomorrow morning to get a head start on the day.

- Make your three lists: long-term projects, short-term projects, and daily to-dos.

- If you struggle with hopping on social media too much, go ahead and download an app that will block those distractions for a set block of time, such as OffTime or Moment. It can't hurt and might help!

CHAPTER 4

ALL THE DON'TS: MISTAKES TO AVOID WHEN WORKING AND LEADING FROM AFAR

few years ago when I was going through post-partum depression, I didn't want to get up. I didn't want to get dressed—and so I didn't. I began to *look* depressed, and everyone in the house got used to that.

Thankfully, I did eventually talk to my doctor, who prescribed medicine that helped pull me out of that hole. As I slowly began to feel more like myself, I did things I knew would make me happy: I got dressed in the morning in clothes that made me feel my best. I did my hair. I began to put on makeup—rendering myself unrecognizable to my family, who, like I said, had gotten used to the other version of me!

But I began to realize that I also had a part in getting myself back together. By listening to what I knew would help restore me, I did more than just let the medicine heal me. I got my confidence back by simply making myself look like myself again. That's what we have to do when we are left to create our own routines.

Do the things that you know will help you be the best version of yourself, that will pull you out of any WFH slump you go through. And yes, that means not working in your pj's—one of the easiest WFH mistakes you can make and yet just as easy to avoid!

That's what we'll cover here over the next few pages: mistakes to avoid when working and leading from afar. Consider this a cheat sheet you can refer to when you need inspiration to get you back on top of your game (and out of those pajamas)!

DON'T NEGLECT YOUR APPEARANCE

The most productive people don't just roll out of bed and start working. They get ready for the day, which includes getting dressed and doing your hair. Take a little bit of time to make yourself presentable as you would if you were in an office environment. I'm not saying every day you need to be in a full face of makeup and business attire, but don't get too comfy.

Home is a place where we are able to relax, yes, but not so much that we are lazy in our physical presentation of ourselves. And as I mentioned before, getting

The most productive people don't just roll out of bed and start working.

dressed for the day also makes you feel good, helps you feel like you've put yourself together, and gives you the mental strength to take on the day.

DON'T IGNORE YOUR FAMILY

While it's best to set aside time to be with your spouse and children away from your office space, we all know things will happen during the day that will still require your attention. Better yet, plan time with them in your schedule before any other activities you need for work. Work will always be there in some form. What the lockdown time with the family showed so many of us is that work isn't everything. I've had to ask myself: "Is it really important for me to be sitting here on my phone at the table with the kids when they're asking me questions? Or can it wait? Do I have to be sending a text message right now? Do I have to be searching, scrolling social media right now when my kids are asking me questions? Or when my husband is asking me a question about dinner?" The answer? No, that text is not important. Take advantage of moments to be *present*.

DON'T LET YOUR BUSINESS RELATIONSHIPS FALL TO THE WAYSIDE

It's easy to get out of the habit of regular face-to-face contact with suppliers and clients when you're suddenly a WFHer. During the coronavirus lockdown, we went from weekly meetings and events to sheltering in place with no roadmap on how to keep those relationships seamlessly afloat. Whether your situation is temporary or permanent, get in the habit of doing frequent video calls to check in and keep building important relationships. What you don't want is for a vendor or employee to feel as though you only call when you need something from them. We have additional responsibilities at home, but make time to build those relationships as you did when in an office. Pick up the phone, write an email, or send a card; just keep in touch (see more resources on this topic on my website).

DON'T WORK IN BED

When you come home, where is the first place that you go to? You pretty much strip off your work clothes, be it a tie or heels, and you go sit on the couch, right? That's your special spot that signals that it's time to take a load off.

Don't work in those relaxing places. Certainly, your designated work space should be comfortable, but working in bed or on the couch will blur the lines between home and work. You want to avoid that at all costs!

DON'T TAKE THE OPPORTUNITY TO WORK FROM HOME FOR GRANTED

Use the time wisely to build up your communication skills (as you have to communicate more and differently) and increase your emotional intelligence (nonverbal cues are hard to pick up on when you are communicating digitally; I have a course for this on my website). Most of us struggle with that, and we've really got to amp up those soft skills since working from home isn't going away anytime soon.

For example, during a recent Zoom call I picked up on a lot of nonverbal cues from colleagues that signaled that several weren't paying attention. I had to make those conclusions and call them out. Use working from home to your advantage by utilizing those additional hours (because you shouldn't be working for the whole eight, remember?). For example, try taking an online course to help advance your knowledge and skills.

DON'T LET YOUR MOOD PLAN YOUR DAY

I have a friend who once told me she didn't understand how I am motivated to go to the gym or work out several days a week. I told her, "Look, if I was dependent on being in the 'mood' to work out, I'd never do it." It's all about getting into a routine and being disciplined enough to stay in it. Don't let your mood, your emotions, or the emotions of others dictate your day, especially when it comes to working from home. Don't forget: when we are at home with our spouses and children, they are watching us.

> Don't forget: when we are at home with our spouses and children, they are watching us.

Emotions can hold us back. We may not *feel* like

doing something that relates to our goal that day. We may *feel* lazy or discouraged or upset that we aren't where we want to be. Taking action reduces those feelings. Taking action is what it takes to fight for your goals.

Discipline is not easy, but it is an engine that helps us understand and explore our capabilities and life's opportunities. Discipline is the freedom to be able to put all of our energy into creating something amazing, meaningful, and beautiful. No one is going to convince you to have discipline or force you to accomplish anything. Having a life of discipline (or not) is completely up to you—just remember, without discipline, achieving your dreams will be nearly impossible!

DON'T WORK ALL DAY AND NIGHT

I have a type-A personality, so many times I feel the need to work most of the day to check things off my list. You may be the same. A deadline may be moved or the workload may unexpectedly increase, and so you have to work, work, work to get it all done. I get it! But if you take a little bit of time, even though you're rushed, to set the priorities, set the strategy, and plan it all out, it's going to be a lot easier on people versus rushing everyone.

Expect things to change and shift throughout the course of a project. Know where you may need to put in additional time to meet the deadlines, but set time limits for yourself so you don't get burned out. For example, I know that I do not work well after 8:30 at night, for sure. I have tried it, and it's just terrible. Know what your good time of day is to work and bust your butt to accomplish your goals during that time. And then we have to have breaks—it's proven that our body needs to take breaks. So don't forget to carve out time for those, too, while avoiding the trap of letting your days bleed into nights.

DON'T FORGET TO REWARD YOURSELF

Gentle reminder once again because it's important: Don't forget to reward yourself. Wrap up a project/ meet a goal and tell yourself that once that's done, you get to have your favorite dessert from your favorite local restaurant, or you get a massage, or you can take yourself and the family out for a movie. Building in both small and big rewards is key. Neglecting to look after yourself is the biggest mistake to avoid, and that's why I want to talk about self-care for the entirety of the following and final chapter.

If you love rewards, you're going to want to stick around and find out how taking care of you is the way to design the best you!

ACTION STEPS

- Reach out to a business relationship and set up a video call to catch up, not just to do business.

- Research ways you can use extra time in your WFH day to up your communication skills. I actually have a set of courses you can check out at **career.vennessamcconkey.com/courses**.

- Set a goal/deadline for a project as well as a reward for its completion, and tell that goal to someone else so you can be held accountable. If it's a massage, go ahead and make that appointment to coincide with the date you plan to meet your goal.

CHAPTER 5

SELF-CARE: DON'T LET WFH LIFE COMPLETELY CONSUME YOU

E very morning, I wake up at 4:30 a.m. Yes, that's early, but it's the time of day that is all mine. I stretch, read, and journal. I meditate and work out. By the time the rest of the family is awake, I'm refreshed, and my mind and body are fresh. I already know what's for breakfast because it's on the family meal calendar I created, knowing that staying organized is also a form of self-care. Otherwise, the week—with a family of five to feed and get ready every day—would be chaos. Instead, I'm ready for the day. I've set myself up for success.

One of my big mottos (and this is after learning the hard way!) is that you can't take care of anyone else until you take care of yourself. Be wary of the temptation to stay in your little corner of the house so much that you neglect yourself. From taking a long weekend break to looking after your nutrition to simply staying properly organized, self-care comes in many forms. It's vital that, in designing the best you—the you that has clarity and confidence every morning and a great work-life balance—you take a moment here and

> One of my big mottos (and this is after learning the hard way!) is that you can't take care of anyone else until you take care of yourself.

there to focus inward. It's in those moments that you can return to your "why," which should be at the center of everything you do.

HAVE SILENT MORNING REFLECTIONS

A moment of silent reflection before you start the day or head into the office will always serve you (and those around you) well. I know you're busy running around and trying to make big things happen, but I'm asking you to give yourself a moment. Even if it's just sitting down for ten minutes with a coffee and a journal or going for a brisk walk around the block before you take on the day, silent reflection will serve you well and help you discover and continuously reflect on your "why": what your goals are, who *you* really are.

Give your mind, body, and soul a chance to feel centered and grounded because all of your power comes from feeling certain and in control. And we can't control what goes on out there in the world, but we can control our own thoughts and attitudes.

Sit down, take out your journal, and write; think about your life and the day ahead. Make your intentions clear and start walking into each new day with a sense of power and purpose within because it is that energy that opportunities and people are attracted to the most.

TAKE A DAY OR TWO

When I say take a break, I don't just mean those little Pomodoro breaks. When working from home, it can become easy to overwork. In particular, leaders feel obligated to always be on. Instead, listen to signs that you need a break like a long weekend away (or even a weekend staycation). It's OK to get away. In fact, it shows your humanity when you're able to step away and focus elsewhere. I do this every quarter—just go stay at a local hotel to rest and rejuvenate.

DON'T SKIP MEALS

Staying properly nourished sets you up for success too. I'm a little bit more aware than most people because of the autoimmune diseases that I handle and whatnot. That's why I love creating a healthy food schedule. Make your own schedule on Sundays, at least planning the breakfast and dinner portions of the weekdays. Invest in healthy snacks, and try to eat something every two or three hours. Set an alarm if needed to remind you to do things like drink more water. Use snack time and lunch time as part of your rewarding Pomodoro breaks.

STAY ORGANIZED

About that calendar! I'm a big fan of having a planner and calendars of all sorts, color-coded calendars at that. Being organized is a form of self-care!

Growing up, my siblings and I had a calendar in the kitchen used to indicate what we were up to after school: a friend's house, a school activity, things like that. It was color-coded, with each kid getting a different color. That sort of laid the foundation for my organizational skills, and to this day, I color-code every planner (and use the color-coded calendar with my family too). Personally, I'm a big fan of Michael Hyatt's Full Focus planner. I will also be releasing my own job search planner in late 2020, which will include all of the healthy advice in this book as well as techniques to have a successful job search.

You can also do that with work tasks, using different colors to reflect the priority level. That way, you can know at a glance what your day is going to look like. My planner is divided into colors reflecting family activities, career coaching, and more. Try it. It helps to keep an otherwise chaotic schedule in some kind of order, be it personal or professional, or both! Some days, you may have a random mix of colors, which is fine, too, but at least you can be mentally prepared for it.

KEEP MOVING

Research has shown that moderate exercise (thirty to ninety minutes most days of the week) increases immune function and relieves stress. With endorphins at work, the benefits are many, from positively impacting our moods and lowering our blood pressure to raising our self-esteem and having a calming effect on our bodies, allowing a deeper, more restful sleep. Whether that's small ten- to fifteen-minute walks throughout the day, a yoga practice, or bike rides to the store, however you can do it, keep moving!

GO OUTSIDE

You can expect to see the same sort of effects, like stress relief and immunity boosts, from going outside as you do from getting ample exercise. Being in nature grounds us. Sunlight provides essential nutrients like Vitamin D, reduces depression, and fights disease. Get that needed outdoor time in small increments throughout your WFH schedule, like meditating in the backyard for five minutes or watering the garden. You can kill a few birds with one stone when it comes to WFH self-care!

LISTEN TO YOUR CREATIVE SIDE

Keep your creative juices flowing, which can inspire both your personal as well as your professional life. What do you enjoy creating? Maybe you enjoy painting, playing an instrument, or making collages— or maybe simply borrowing your kid's coloring book will do the trick! Whatever it is, tap into a creative activity that calms you, inspires you, and makes you smile.

HAVE CONVERSATIONS

Don't get too isolated when working from home. We all need to hear the human voice. Even if you can't meet up with someone, a video coffee chat can be so energizing and great for your soul. I don't just mean colleagues—make sure you don't get so isolated that you forget to connect with the people you love. Schedule it in your calendar if you have to!

> Don't get too isolated when working from home. We all need to hear the human voice.

Even better, go outside when you'd normally come home from work. Disconnect. Say hi to a neighbor. Walk with your spouse or kids. Cut out the noise and have conversations.

DECLUTTER

Keep your space clear of chaos. It's easy for your dedicated WFH space to become cluttered, what with the fact it may also be your bedroom or kid's room. Spending a few minutes tidying up can go a long way in helping you have the clarity to start the day. It sounds crazy but it's true: when your space is a mess, your brain tends to feel a little messy too.

Work-life balance is the key: you need time to do great work and live a great life. That means taking breaks, spending time with family, and always going back to your *why*.

This is your life, so start creating the life you actually *want* to live and start doing things your way. *You* are the most important person, and you have to give yourself time to work out what that actually looks and feels like. You also have to allow time for those things that empower you and nourish your soul.

ACTION STEPS

- Get a journal (I've been using the Full Focus Planner by Michael Hyatt for years) and start spending a few minutes every morning setting some intentions. Check back in with yourself in a week and make it a point to observe how that practice has been of benefit. You can access free journal prompts on my website at **career.vennessamcconkey.com/ free-journal-prompts**.

- Try color-coding your planner with the following week's tasks. Hopefully, you'll see the same chaos-free results many of my clients experience. Go to **vennessamcconkey.com** to see examples of what my calendar looks like some weeks, and send me a photo of yours when you're done. I just might feature yours on my social media channels!

- Find a creative activity you can tap into this week—something opposite of the work you do!

CONCLUSION

BE THE BEST YOU AND HAVE A GREAT LIFE

Whether COVID-19 landed you in a WFH position or you've intentionally placed yourself there, you have the power to set yourself up for success in the comfort of your home. Grab hold of the new WFH normal we're encountering and realize that not only is it likely here to stay, but it's also a gift. Seize it as an opportunity to create a WFH environment that you love, surrounding yourself with everything you need to confidently work and lead from afar.

Realizing that the eight-hour workday is a myth, use that extra time for improvement in everything from working more efficiently and doing what truly energizes you to spending time with your family and nurturing yourself a little more. This is a chance for a brand-new mindset that allows you the space to gain more clarity and confidence in your career while also seeing to it that you're living your best home life too. That can be a feat when working from home, but it's yours to conquer!

A good work-life balance is key to designing the best you—you just need to be focused, consistent, and deliberate in achieving it. OK, guys, you know what to do now. Get back to work on designing the best *you* because there's only one YOU designed to serve this world.

DESIGN YOUR
CAREER TODAY!

Visit **vennessamcconkey.com** for resources you need to level up your career and be a valuable asset to your organization!

RESOURCES

Go to **vennessamcconkey.com/pages/resources** to check out all the links mentioned in this book, as well as templates you need in your job search!

DESIGNING THE BEST YOU COURSE

This course was designed specifically with YOU in mind. If you are a busy professional but need help with kick-starting and streamlining your job search, this course is for you! You have the opportunity to watch the videos and use the templates at your own pace, any time of day that is convenient for YOU! Find more info at **vennessamcconkey.com/pages/ diy-course-page**.

1:1 CAREER COACHING

If you are ready to dive in and massively change your career, whether within your current role or transitioning into a new role, then let's get you into career coaching sessions. In three months, you'll have more clarity, know how to brand and market yourself, and gain that confidence you need! Schedule your FREE consultation: **vennessamcconkey.com/pages/ one-on-one-coaching**.

JOB SEARCH PLANNER

What everyone has been BEGGING for is now a reality! This job search planner isn't your ordinary planner. This planner is designed with the job seeker in mind. There's been no "book of job searching" created. How do you know what to do, how often to do it, and when in your job search? Well, this planner *is* that guide! Find it on my resource page: **vennessamcconkey.com/pages/resources**.

MY PODCAST: *DESIGNING THE BEST YOU!*

Want to listen in on some nuggets of advice and wisdom from myself and other powerful career leaders? Make sure to subscribe and leave a five-star review too! Search "Designing the Best You podcast" or go to: **vennessamcconkey.com/pages/podcast**.

ABOUT THE AUTHOR

Vennessa McConkey is a career coach, owner, and founder of Vennessa McConkey Coaching and Top Line Resumes LLC, cofounder of ElevateUp LLC, speaker, and podcast host of *Designing the Best YOU!* She is on a mission to give professionals clarity, confidence, focus, and tools they need to stop all the frenzy in their lives so they can be all they were created to be. Over the course of her career, she quickly advanced in traditional corporate jobs (including time in engineering, quality, operations, and marketing roles within the manufacturing, dental, precision machining, and steel fabrication industries).

Through her work as an executive coach, she has formally and informally helped hundreds of clients, colleagues, and friends find job satisfaction—whether they chose to uplevel within their current company, find a new job, or completely change careers. Vennessa's work has been featured in Ladders, LinkedIn features, and more, as well as on multiple podcasts and stages covering career, success, health, and designing the best you.

Why does she work so hard? First of all, she loves to serve—in all areas of life. Second, her three boys and husband are her world. Third, having an incredible career with minimal stress is incredibly important, as she knows all too well how health can be seriously affected if parts of life are out of whack.

9 781642 252071